Akin to Stone

Tenin Taşa Yakınlığı

Bejan Matur

Akin to Stone
Tenin Taşa Yakınlığı

Translated from Turkish by
Jen Hadfield and Canan Marasligil

poetry
translation
centre

First published in 2020
by the Poetry Translation Centre Ltd
The Albany, Douglas Way, London, SE8 4AG

www.poetrytranslation.org

Poems © Bejan Matur 2017
English Translations © Jen Hadfield and Canan Marasligil 2020
Introduction © Canan Marasligil 2020
Afterword © Malika Booker 2020

Some of these poems and translations first appeared in *If This is a Lament* (Poetry Translation Centre; 2017).

ISBN: 978-1-9161141-0-4

A catalogue record for this book is available from the British Library

Typeset in Minion by Poetry Translation Centre Ltd

Series Editor: Edward Doegar
Cover Design: Kit Humphrey
Printed in the UK by T.J. International

The PTC is supported using public funding by
Arts Council England

Contents

Introduction	7
If this is a lament	13
Truth	15
Lalesh	17
Glacier	21
Shadow	23
Full moon over Karbala	25
Growing up in two dreams	27
In the temple of a patient god	31
That smile is creation	33
Earth's dream	35
A Dead Sun	37
There is no spring	39
Every woman knows her own tree	41
A soul growing cold	43

Ceremonial robes	45
Dark Rain	49
I've learnt –	51
Requiem for Saroyan	53
Afterword	59
About the contributors	64
About the series	66

Introduction

A young girl smiles beyond valleys on a world that doesn't smile back. Her smile is creation, as the title of the poem these verses are taken from suggests. They capture the intention and depth of Bejan Matur's poetry, and her ongoing attempt, like the girl in her poem (perhaps her own self) to create in the face of violence and death, a space for the imagination where poetry becomes survival.

Bejan Matur is an award-winning Kurdish-Alevi poet from Turkey writing in Turkish and Kurdish. Her poetry has been translated into more than twenty-seven languages.

Her father wanted her to become a lawyer, or a journalist. She graduated from law school but, having seen injustice routinely meted out across her country under the banner of the law – and experiencing it firsthand when she was tortured in prison in 1988 – she grew disillusioned with the profession. She reflects that if she had pursued a legal career, today she would be a human rights lawyer.

What Bejan Matur does as a writer, columnist and poet may not serve a legal function, but it is a form of advocacy: for human rights in general, for the Kurdish people and also for the rights of women and other minority and threatened groups in Turkey. The gesture of writing and reading poetry is a necessity both for the poet and for the reader.

The poems in this book, a revised edition from previously published *If This is a Lament* (2017) with additional poems now presented under the title *Akin to Stone*, are deeply rooted in the historical, cultural and political context of the Kurdish people of Turkey. The 'Kurdish question', as it is usually referred to in the Turkish media and in mainstream narratives, has been ongoing for four decades. It is an armed conflict between the Turkish state and various Kurdish insurgent groups. One side claims that they fight for their freedom and the other side brands them as terrorists and separatists. The polarised discourses resulting from the issue alarmingly grow in Turkey and beyond. While it is far too complex a reality to explain in a short introduction, it is important to acknowledge this context as the fraught territory from which Matur's poetry emerges and which it transcends.

Matur's poems depict a lot of pain, blood and suffering, but she abhors victimization, instead carving out a space to dream, to create, to hope and to love. Her poetry is spiritual, almost mystical, though not religious. While she does mention 'god' in certain poems, the holiness she seeks through her poetry derives from and is situated in the heart – the poet's heart, which reaches towards truth, as we read in 'Ceremonial Robes':

> Perhaps history is a mistake, the poet says.
> *Humankind is a mistake*, says god.

This particular brand of spirituality can also be found in Matur's depictions of nature and the rural landscapes of Kurdistan, within and beyond the borders of Turkey. The mountains, the rivers, the moon, the sun and the vegetation all give rhythm to her verses. In her poems, words yearn for a summit, they flow, they shine, they breathe in synchrony with the wind. They are also deeply connected to the self, the body and humanity, as can be seen in the first lines of 'Requiem for Saroyan'.

Bejan Matur has always moved from place to place – within Turkey as a child and young woman, and subsequently in Europe and across the world. She has lived in many geographies but her poetry is deeply rooted in the region where she was born, to its landscapes, its history, its cultures and emotions.

Some events are so harrowing that they change one's whole understanding of history and humanity. Matur was ten years old in 1978, when neo-fascist and religious conservative groups orchestrated a pogrom against the Alevis in her native city. The Maraş Massacre showed her a world which was a battleground between 'us' and 'them'. She began to wonder: why are they killing us? You can feel the constant presence of this essential and impossible question, with all its philosophical underpinnings, throughout Bejan Matur's poetic oeuvre.

Perhaps, as the poem 'Shadow' suggests poetry becomes a construction, against all odds, of a reclaimed memory:

> Now we're going back to the source,
> back to our roots.
> Alone in the history of our tribe and race.
> Melancholy waits
> at the top of the mountain –
> it's the past's grief
> not ours –

Through her verses Bejan Matur creates a connection between reality and the imagination, between memory and the present, between the stone and the skin. Her poetry is an invitation: to feel, to ponder and to express humanity with beauty.

Canan Marasligil

Poems

Bir ağıtsa bu

Olmayan bir ülkeden söz ediyorlar
Olmayan dilden, kardeşlikten.
Konuşma yok
Yok kelimeler.

Anlaşılmak içinse yeryüzü
Kim ölümü anlatacak
Dağların aldığı nefesi
Çöken karanlığı
Kim anlatacak,
Bir çocuğun rüyasında büyüyenleri
Kim?

Kuşların kanatları
Eski bir masaldan bana doğru çırpınıyor
Eski kadınların anlattığı
Tenin taşa yakınlığı.

Belli ki bir ağıtçıyım ben,
Karanlık çöktüğünde
Dağların ötesinde
Kimi ansam bakıyor bana acıyla.

Bu bir ağıtsa
Ağlamak henüz başlamadı.

If this is a lament

They speak of a land that never was,
a non-existent tongue.
There is no utterance,
no words.

If we're put on earth
to understand each other –
who can make sense of death?

Explain how the mountains stole breath,
or translate the darkness
that has fallen?

Who can say what burgeons
in a child's dream?

Flapping out of an ancient tale,
birds' wings bear down
on me – and skins

akin to stone
as the old women used to say.
When darkness falls

beyond the mountains,
the people I remember look to me
in pain. My words are elegy.

If this is a lament,
we haven't even
begun to cry.

Hakikat

Taşların bildiği
İnsanın unuttuğu

Truth

What stones know
                humankind
forgets

Laleş

Bu güneştir
Bu da ev.
Meleğin koruduğu yuva
Bekler hep.

Diyor ki bana
Eşiklerden geçerek
Gör siyah olanı
İnsanlığı kurtaranı gör.
Hani o yükseklikten
Dağların insanı koruyan vakarından
Söz eden.
Başlıyorum düğümlerden
Kumaşların dileklerle mühürlendiği
Karanlıktan başlıyorum.
Ve batıyor güneşimiz bizim
Herkesten önce.
Çocukların vaftizi
Badem ağaçlarına
Asılmış dilek.
Bahar geldi
Ve gidişin senin
Bitmedi hiç.

Bana diyor ki
Gözyaşlarının soğukluğunu

Lalesh

This is the sun.
And I am home. The nest
the peacock angel protects

waiting faithfully.
The man tells me –

*Look, see the Black One
who hovers on the thresholds.
See the One who can save humanity...*

He tells how human dignity
was preserved by the height
of these mountains.

He says *Our sun is the first to set.
The baptism of children is a wish
hung on almond trees.*

I start on the knots.
I begin in the dark, untying
wishes sealed into velvet.

Spring has come –
and your departure is
never-ending.

Kapıda bırak.
O bizim borcumuzdur.
Unutma diyor
Evin bu dağların yanı.
Seni inananların sabahında
En önde ağırlayacağız
Kızıl kadifeler içinde
Badem ağaçlarına ve taşlara sunarak
Ve bilerek hangi acı karartmamış yürekleri.

Ben gizli bir inanandım
Ve gizli kaldım.
Sırrım çözüldü ve
O dağın kovuğunda
Bulduğum acıdan saadet
Ve benzerliğim onlara,
Evet yuvayadır dönüş
Ve yuva
Dağların arasında unutulmuş
Badem ağaçları
Ve düğümlerdir.

Laleş 1 Mart 2014

He tells me –
Leave your cold tears at the door.
This is our burden.

Don't forget –
You belong here by the mountains.
In the morning we will welcome you...

Making offerings to
almond trees and stones,
in scarlet velvet,

hearts undimmed by pain,
they recognised me –
a secret believer.

I found calm sorrow in the mountain's den.

And yes – I will come home,
to the almond trees and those knots
forgotten in the mountains.

1 March 2014, Lalesh

Buzul

O gölde buzlarla çevrilmiş, binlerce yıldır ölüydüm.
Uyandırdın.
Uyandım ve yanmış bir ormanın sisinde buldum uykumu.
Geceye yapıştı gövdem.

Bir buzulun derin ışığından tene akan beyazlık
Hatırlattı;

O gölde yürüdün sen.
Ten ve iz bırakarak.

Glacier

Dead to the world a thousand years,
in a lake immured in ice.

You woke me up.

Mist. I found I'd been sleeping
in a charred forest.

My body clung to night.

White light from the depth of the glacier
floods into my skin,
reminds me –

you walked on that lake.
Leaving your tracks – skin, scars.

Gölge

Mor dağların gölgesi
Ve unutkanlık
Daha fazlası yok,
Vadilerin uğultusu
Ve ağrıyan kalbim.
Asıl şimdi
Başa dönüyoruz
Aşiret ve soy tarihinde yalnız,
Bu dağ başında
Bulduğumuz hüzün
Bizim değil
Geçmişin…

Shadow

The velvet shadow of mountains
forgetfulness
and nothing more –
humming of valleys
my aching heart.
Now we're going back to the source,
back to our roots.
Alone in the history of our tribe and race.
Melancholy waits
at the top of the mountain –
it's the past's grief
not ours –

Kerbela dolunayı

Ve ay
Unutmak tepelerinden
Yükseliyor üzerimize,
Tarihte ilerleyen adanmışları gösteriyor
Yanılmış bir göğün altında beklerken
Sebepleri bilen ve susan.

Full moon over Karbala

And above us
the moon
climbs clear of the summits of
forgetfulness
to show the faithful marching on
under their misleading sky
which does
know why –
but does not speak
out

İki rüyada büyümek

Sen uykudan söz ederken
İki rüyada büyümüş biri gibi
Kalbim bölünüyor.
Duvara yansıyan ışığın
Yaptığı kelimeler,
O kelimeler
Uykuda geldiği için belki de
Hâlâ dönüyorlar etrafımda.
Bana dağları anlatıyorlar
İnanmanın kanıyla ayakta duran
Dağları.

Çünkü bir sabahtır sonunda
Bizi uyandıracak olan.
Elimizden alınmış dünya ve doğumla
Bir dağ yolunda ilerlerken sen
Bacası tüten bir ev
Sulardan geçip gitmekte olan renk
Anlatmaz yine de
Olanı,
Bize konuşanı
Kimdir?

Growing up in two dreams

While you talk about sleep like someone
who grew up in two dreams
my heart splits.

The light reflected on the wall makes words –
perhaps while I slept they appeared –
still swirling around me.
Mountains, they say
*the mountains stand still
with the blood of belief.*

Because it's morning after all
that will shake us awake.
Earth and our birth-right
have been stolen.

You walk a mountain road.
A house with a smoking chimney –
like colour dispersing in water –
doesn't tell the truth.

The one speaking to us
is still invisible.
Who is it?

Çünkü tarih açmıştır yaraları bir kez
Öfkenin bağladığı kabuklar
İncelmiştir çoktan.

Artık yalnızca sese sığınıyoruz
Işıklı geceye.
Kime gideceğiz,
Hangi sözle anlatacağız acıyı,
Hangi dilde bağışlanmayı dileyeceğiz?
Bize saf bir başlangıç gerekli
Kelimelerin gün doğumunda
Ruha bağlandığı bir başlangıç.
Bize bir yuvanın şefkati gerekli,
Kıyısından geçerken bacası tüten bir ev ki
Affetmenin toprağında
Sığınılacak bir yurt zannedip
Susalım
Susalım.

History has already opened these wounds.
Fragile, the scars, thickened
with anger.

Our voices are our only shelter in the lit night.
Who can we turn to?
What words can we use to speak of pain,
in what language can we ask to be forgiven?
We need a clean slate,
a sunrise of words,
dawn of the soul.

We need the gentle home with chimney smoking.
To walk by its walls on forgiving soil.
We decide this is somewhere
we can take refuge
and fall quiet
we fall quiet

Sabır tanrısının tapinağinda konaklama

I.

Yağmurlu dağların arasından gurbetini seçtin.

Son gece beklediğin yer
Sabır tanrısının eviydi.
İnsanı merhametle donatmanın evi.
Tapınaklara gerek yok dedim.
Burası sadece bir yer.
İnsanın ruhu tapınak kılınmalı.
Ve yağmur, yersizliğin nehri.
Tanrıdan ve çocukluktan hatırlanan

II.

Yağmurlu dağların arasından gurbetini seçtin.

Yanılmanın güzelliği
Ve huzuru acının.
Her şey seni bir boşluğa uladı.
Ve sen, sarı sabır çiçeklerine bakıp ağladın.
Onun koynunda yokmuş gibi uyudun.
Bir dağa gidilecek, gurbet seçilecek.
Ve insan istenecek tanrıdan.

Tekrar dinlemeli o müziği.
Sevişmenin tamamlanmadığı o yer.

In the temple of a patient god

I.

You chose exile in rain-drenched mountains.

You stayed in the house of a patient god
and were adorned with grace.

What do we need with temples? I said –
this is just a place.

Make the human soul the sacred space;
rain, the rootless river, remembered
from god and childhood.

II.

You chose exile in rain-swept mountains.

It all leads to the void –
the beauty of delusion and
the peace of pain.

As for you, you observed
the serenity of primroses, and wept.
Drifted off in his arms, as if you didn't exist.

A journey shall be made to the mountains.
We can ask god to send us
a human: a sign.

Let's listen to that music again.
Return to the place where we're still making love.

O gülüş yaradılıştır

Bir kız çocuğunun
Vadileri aşan gülümsemesi
Ve gözleri bir kız çocuğunun,
Ona gülmeyen hayata gülümsemesi.
O gülüş yaradılıştır.
Dünyaya mı,
Ölüme mi bakmaktadır
Belli değil.

That smile is creation

That wee lass's smile
reaches far beyond the valleys.
And her eyes
are smiling on a world
that doesn't smile back.
That smile is creation.
Is it life she's smiling at –
or death?
It's uncertain –

Yeryüzünün Düşü

Göğün gecesi yalnızken
Düşünmüş,
Bu yıldızlar niçin?
Neden içimin karanlığında uğuldayan bu ses?
Sesler çekilse
Ne kalır
Ruhumu kemiren boğuntudan geriye?

Kutup yıldızı yerinden oynasa bir an,
Balıkçı mı şaşırır yolunu,
Çoban mı unutur ıslığını?
Belki de hiçbir şey,
Hiçbir şey hakikatimi değiştirmez.
Yeryüzünün düşüyüm ben
Uykusunu bitiren insan
Uyanınca görecek
Asıl karanlık ötede.

Earth's dream

In its loneliness, the night sky thought –
Why these stars?

Whose voice hums in the heart
of my darkness?

If it ever stops,
what will be left but suffocation
gnawing at my soul?

If the Pole Star is knocked one second off
its mark, is the fisherman lost?

Will the shepherd forget his whistle?

Maybe nothing
can alter my truth.

I am the earth's dream.

A sleeper waking
will see what lies beyond –
true darkness

Ölü bir güneş

Geceyi
Ölmüş bir güneşin teninden kazıyıp
Geçirdim yüreğime.

A Dead Sun

I peel night
from the dead sun's flesh
and like a scarf
wrap it round
my heart

Bahar yok

Erguvanlar açmış
Yastayız yine
Bahar yok
Ülke yok
Ve her yer kan içinde.

There is no spring

The Judas trees are blossoming.
We're in mourning again.
There is no spring the
fertile land is
drowning in
blood.

Her kadın kendi ağacını tanır

Sana geldiğimde
Kanatlarımı,
Siyah taşlarla örülmüş
O ıssız şehrin üzerinde açacak,
Bulduğum bir ağacın dallarına tüneyecek
Ve acıyla bağıracaktım.

Her kadın kendi ağacını tanır.

Uçtum o gece.
Karanlığın girmeye korktuğu şehri geçtim.
Gölge olmayınca ruh yalnızdı. Uludum.

Every woman knows her own tree

When I looked for you
I spread my wings over the city
built of black, abandoned stones,
found a tree and perched on its boughs
and shrieked with pain.

Every woman knows her own tree.

That night, I crossed a city
so black that darkness
feared to enter it.

My soul was lonely
without its shadow.

I howled.

Bir ruhun soğuması

Büyük bir kâinatı geçtim denizinde ben.
Ona, bir gölgeden başlayarak oluşan ruhu gösterdim.
Kanlı bir deniz ve yeryüzü sanılan boşluk.
Boşlukta kımıldayan dünya.
Şimdi kanatsızım.
Kesik yerinden damlayan kanı, dalgalar emdi.
Ona bir ruhun soğumasını göstereceğim.
Çocuk olmayı ve anneyi beklemeden karanlıkta uyumayı.

A soul growing cold

I crossed a universe – an infinite sea.
I showed him soul
evolving from shadow.

Ocean of blood; and
shivering in emptiness,
what we used to call
The World.

Now, I have no wings.
Waves lap the blood
flowing from the wound.

I am going to show him a soul
growing cold. Becoming

a child in the dark.
Putting herself to sleep,
not waiting for her mother.

Tören giysileri

Çürümüş donuk kalbinde bu toprakların
Gözleri gördüm.
Herkes sesiyle vardı
Ve duruşuyla gövdesinin.
Bir insanı en iyi sevişirken tanırız.
Kalbimizi birlikte çürütürken.
Ağırlaşan gövdemiz
Gece uyandırır.
Mezar gibidir avlulu evler.
Çocukluk bir uykudur. Uzun sürer.
Ve dokunmak için bir arzu
Bir arzu sürükler bizi ölüme.
Ben kendimi sınadım her gövdede
Ben kendimi bıraktım her şehirde
İçime aldım göğünü ülkelerin
Ve boşluğunu görünce kalbimin
Gitmeli dedim.

Çürümüş tören giysileri içinde
Askıda salınan kökler.
Biz denize düşürsek de ateşi
O hep yanar.
Issızlık bahşeder karanlığa. Yanar.
Tarih bir yanılgı olabilir diyor şair
İnsan bir yanılgıdır diyor tanrı.
Çok sonra
Bu toprakların kalbi kadar

Ceremonial robes

In the cold dead heart of the land
I saw their eyes. Everyone
was there, with their own stance and voice.
We know each other best when we make love:
together, our hearts decay.

Our bodies, growing heavy, wake us in the night.
Houses with courtyards are like graves.
Childhood is a slumber. It lasts a long
time. And the desire to touch
hauls us towards death.

I tried myself in every
body. Lost myself in every city,
took each country's sky to heart –
and when I saw the emptiness of my heart –
that's enough, I said.

Inside decaying ceremonial robes,
roots swaying on the hanger.
Even if we douse it in the sea.
this fire will burn forever.
It beats out light in the darkness.
It burns on.

Perhaps history is a mistake, the poet says.
Humankind is a mistake, says god.

Çürümüş bir sonrada
İnsan bir yanılgıdır diyor tanrı.
Ve düzeltmek için varım
Ama geciktim.

Ölü kızıl suyun dalgası
Gece yürünen yol
Ve yolcuların dağıldığı zavallı yeryüzü
Salınan beyaz kefenler
Tören giysileri.
Ve bir koşu için gerekli tek şey
Atın yelesidir.
Aslolan,
Şimdi ve burada
Çürüyüp kaldık.

Tanrı görmesin harflerimi
İnsan bir hata diyor durmadan
Ve hatasını düzeltmek için
Acı veriyor
Sadece acı.

Şubat 1997, Berlin

The future is corrupt
as the heart of the land.
Humans are a mistake, says god.
I have come to put things right
but too late.

Red tide of the dead –
the road taken at night.
And the poor earth where pilgrims scatter.
Wan shrouds sweeping – ceremonial robes.

To flee, we need
the horse's mane.

This is the truth:
left here, we rot.

May god not read my words.
He keeps saying *humankind*
was a mistake. And correcting himself
brings sorrow, nothing
but sorrow.

February 1997, Berlin

Kara bir yağmur

Ört üstümü.
Kabuk değiştireyim.
Gün gibi, kuşları gibi sabahın.
Kara bir yağmur yağarken.

Dark Rain

Cover me up
so I can shed my skin.
Like morning birds
when a dark
rain falls.

Dünyada olmak acıdır. Öğrendim.

Yeryüzündeki tüm kızıl taşlara
Tanrının kanı sürülmüştür.
Bu yüzden kızıl taşlar
Çocukluğumuzu öğretir.
Tanrı, biz çocukken,
Yanımızda dolaşır.
Küpemize dokunur
Ve kolyemize.
Pabuçlarımıza ve kurdelamızın
Kızçocuk olmak kıvrımına girer
Saklanır.

Kızıl bir elbise ve yatak almalıyım,
Kızıl bir yüzük,
Ve lamba.
O zaman olmalı ki,
Annenin zamanı başlar ve tükenir.

Beklemeyi bilen kan,
Taş olmayı da bilir.
Dünyada olmak acıdır. Öğrendim.

Kızıl karanlık
Mavi karanlık
Ve başlangıç
Bir anlamı olmalı ki bunların,
Bırakmaz bizi annemiz ve tanrımız.

I've learnt –

on every single red stone on earth,
the blood of god was smeared.
That's how red stones
teach us our childhood.
When we're children, god
walks alongside us.
He toys with our earrings
and our necklaces.
He plays hide-and-seek in our ribbons and shoes,
entering the fold of our girlhood.

I will buy a red dress and bed,
a red ring and lamp.

The mother's time comes – and
will come to an end.

Blood knows how to wait,
how to turn to stone.
I've learnt –
to be in the world is pain.

Blood darkness,
bruise darkness,
and the beginning –
they whisper to us –
we won't be abandoned
by our mother,
our god

Saroyan'a Ağıt

Bitlis'in dağları kar içinde
Dağları Bitlis'in ah
Geçmişin.
Bir adamın yurdunu ararken
Bulduğu taşlar
Taş mıdır sadece?

Yas içinde bir kadın
Bir gömleği taşıyor
Acıdan bir gömleği anlatıyor bize.
Bakın diyor dağlar hâlâ soğuk
Bakın kartallar
Geyikler
Ve meşe
Biz unutmadık.

Göğsünde
Bir yastan kalan kederle
Yakıştın gecemize
Yakıştın toprakta büyüyen yalnızlığa.
Senin dönüşüne bakıyorum ben
Bitlis'in dağlarına
Bir babanın kanlı başını süsleyen güllerin
Solmadığı zamana
Bakıyorum inatla.

Requiem for Saroyan

The mountains of Bitlis are covered in snow
the mountains of Bitlis,
oh – the past.
The man looking for his homeland –
are the stones he finds
just stones?

A woman in mourning
is carrying a shirt.
She tells us the shirt is filled with pain.
Look – she says – *in the mountains, it's still cold.*
Look – eagles
oak-trees
and deer.
We won't forget.

With the grief from her lament
still lingering in your breast,
you belong in our night.
You belong in the loneliness growing in our soil.
I watch for your return
to the mountains of Bitlis,
stubbornly, I look
to the time when the roses
that dress a father's bloody head
don't fade.

Ve biliyorum
Aynı kelimeler
Aynı yerden söylense de
Aynı dağları
Aynı vadileri
Anlatmaz
Ve nehri özlemenin
Aynı uzaklığa ulaşmaz.

Şimdi bir müziğin
Her şeyi yenilediği
Bu sabah,
Bir adamın
Bir taşın karşısında
Oturmasıdır geçmiş.
Harfleri okunmayan
Kırık bütün kalpler gibi
Acı içinde
Bir taş.

Ceplerine taş dolduran adamı
Hatırladın mı
Bir yurt arayan üzgün adamı
Onun yaslandığı duvar
Onun baktığı rüzgâr
Taş toplamaktadır hâlâ bellekte
Bellekte taş sökmektedir

And I know
we can't use the same words
to speak of the same mountains
and the river of longing will never
attain the same valleys.

This morning,
one music renews everything –
history is a man
sitting in front of a shattered
stone – indecipherable,
and like all broken hearts –
a stone
in pain.

Do you remember
the man filling his pockets with stones,
the desolate man searching for his homeland?
He's leaning on the wall.
He's looking at the wind.

When we remember him,
he is still gathering stones.

When we remember him,
he's still dismantling stones.

Because there lies
ahead of us a journey
greater than death,

Çünkü ölümden daha büyük
Bir yol var önümüzde
Artık karları bağışlıyorum
Kışta tükenen soluğu, gidişi
Artık her şeyi bağışlıyorum

now I forgive the snows,
the departure,
the last breath

stolen by winter,
– now
I forgive everything

Afterword

Akin to Stone is an astonishingly powerful collection. Bejan Matur forges an imaginative reincarnation and re-imagining of the historical, cultural and political upheavals of the Kurdish people in Turkey through the poems of searing lyric intensity. Matur's work reads, on the one hand, as a sublime utterance of desolation and loss, while, on the other, creating a testimony to the silencing and unarticulated impact of individual and collective atrocities.

This attempt to translate the human suffering of a people and its psychological effects through the poetic imagination adds a unique voice to the rich tradition of 'poetry of witness'. It is a voice grappling with the uncertainty of lyric as means of testimony, lament and chronicle. It is unafraid to expose and express these trepidations within the poems themselves.

The first poem in the collection, 'If this is a lament', can be read as an assertion and/or enquiry. It is, at once, a statement of bold intent and acknowledgement of nebulous uncertainty. The poem serves to establish Matur's modus operandi – her inimitable poetics of negation. Throughout the collection she presents an image then subverts it with a negative creating a sense of formal inevitability that recalls the processing of a photograph. The effect is to eloquently conjure up darkness and absence, the elements by which we recognise the presence of trauma, and which serve as recurring themes throughout the collection.

The first four verses of that opening poem, 'If this is a lament', introduce a litany of impossible rhetorical statement/questions, opening out from its undecided title:

> They speak of a land that never was,
> a non-existent tongue.

> There is no utterance,
> no words.
>
> If we're put on earth
> to understand each other –
> who can make sense of death?

The conditional mood of the sentences and the paradoxical construction highlight the urgency of this poet's impossible task, to make absence present. The lines invite an attentiveness from the reader, set up the poet's ambitions and parameters, as well as preparing the impossible, insurmountable challenge of this lyrical undertaking. This initial poem works as a manifesto of sorts, an introduction to Matur's poetics and an establishment of the notion of 'the missing'. A close reading of its questions serves to illuminate the poetics of negation where the shadow is placed in the foreground.

In the poem 'Growing up in two dreams' Matur again employs this rhetorical form of reasoning turned back on itself, where she questions the validity and impossibility of using language to translate a fraught silence by asking:

> What words can we use to speak of pain,
> In what language can we ask to be forgiven?

or in the poem 'Earth's Dream':

> Whose voice hums in the heart
> of my darkness?

or, again, in 'Requiem for Soroyan':

> The man looking for his homeland –
> are the stones he finds
> just stones?

an idea the poet returns to, this over-freighting of the landscape and its nouns with an unutterable meaning.

Alongside this poetics of negation, as I have called Matur's approach, these examples illuminate and dismantle the lyric urge towards intense polarities. Matur's grammatical nuance allows her to question as well as embody such intensities. Towards the end of 'If this is a lament' we seem to reach a point of emphatic certainty, 'My words are elegy', only for Matur to disavow or distort the claim by repeating the title as a conditional refrain: 'My words are elegy. // If this is a lament'. The close proximity and juxtaposition of these lines create an unsettling paradox, reinforced further by the concluding lines: 'we haven't even / begun to cry.'

The Romanian Jewish poet Paul Celan found that the only way to articulate experiences of the Shoah was through an metaphorical landscape rich in ambiguity and dichotomy. In his poem 'Death Fugue' ('Todesfuge'), Celan employs images constructed through the radical juxtaposition of contrast, in an attempt to engage the reader with an unimaginable horrific terrain. Matur also draws on this tradition by constructing images of binary opposition in sense and logic in the same sentence. The consequences of imagination, of being able to think something and so make it possible, seems to haunt lines like 'Houses with courtyards are like graves'. In the poem 'Ceremonial robes', the couplet 'We know each other best when we make love: / together, our hearts decay' establishes an emotional resonance through the positivity of its key words – best, make love, together, hearts – which is then undercut by the close proximity of heart to decay. This becomes a familiar trope in the collection in lines like 'you belong in the loneliness growing in our soil' or 'I look / to the time when the roses / that dress a father's bloody head / don't fade' ('Requiem for Saroyan'). There is always a surreal impossibility within the textual image that invites an emotive response as well as a sense of the shadows: loss, grief, and missing. The unity of Matur's poetic voice and the purpose with which she pursues this is astonishing.

In the poem 'Earth's dream' Matur departs from what I have described as her poetics of negation. Here, she employs illusive imagery and juggles the sensory and the sensible: 'In its loneliness, the night sky thought – / Why these stars?' This colossal religious/philosophical querying both includes and exceeds the human: 'If the Pole Star is knocked one second off / its mark, is the fisherman lost?' These questions build and build, to culminate in the declarative statement: 'I am the earth's dream'. But we, as her readers, are encouraged to contemplate, as a 'sleeper waking' what 'true darkness' might be.

Perhaps the poem 'Lalesh' represents the longest respite in this haunting collection. It is a poem of place that is at once historical testimony, homage and a moment of light in a collection where the emblematic repeating images have been represented by 'night' and 'shadows', by an articulated absence.

Matur breaks this from the first line where she establishes the Temple of Lalesh and its three surrounding mountains as the 'sun,' from the first verse:

This is the sun.
And I am home. The nest
the peacock angel protects

alluding to the historical moment in 2014 when over 50,000 Yazidis refugees fled persecution and sheltered in the temple and mountains. The imagery in this remembrance poem is drawn from the origin stories, legends, poems and songs passed down orally about this place. It's power lies in the cultural specificity and significance of the imagery. For instance, 'peacock angel' alludes to the fact that when God created the universe its protection was entrusted to seven angels and the primary angel was incarnated into the body of a peacock. This poem breaks from the self-silencing encountered in previous poems such as 'Growing up in two dreams' where the acknowledged safe-haven of speech, 'Our voices are our only shelter in the lit night', is tested by the lines that follow:

> we decide this is somewhere
> we can take refuge
> and fall quiet
> we fall quiet

The pathos lies in the last three lines reinforced by that decisively loud repetition of 'quiet'. Through these strategies of contradiction Matur makes the paradoxical possible, she gives voice to the unspeakable. It is because of this that the poetry in *Akin to Stone* is so necessary. It is a nuanced work, of mesmerising disquiet.

Malika Booker

Bejan Matur is multi-award-winning Kurdish poet and writer. She is a leading figure in the bold new women's poetry emerging from the Middle East. Her poetry engages directly with the struggles of her people, and yet there is also a mysticism in her writing, a closeness to nature, an embracing of mythology. Her first collection of poetry, *Rüzgar Dolu Konaklar* (*Winds Howl Through the Mansions*, 1996), won several literary prizes. She is the author of eight further collections including: *Tanrı Görmesin Harflerimi* (*God Must Not See the Letter of My Script*, 1999); *Ayın Büyüttüğü Oğullar* (*The Sons Reared by the Moon*, 2002) and *İbrahim'in Beni Terketmesi* (*How Abraham Abandoned Me*, 2008). Her poetry has been translated into 27 languages and she has taught on the International Writing Program at the University of Iowa. She has also written prose books and works for the stage.

Jen Hadfield was born in Cheshire and lives in Shetland, whose landscape and natural life persistently informs her work. Her second poetry book *Nigh-No-Place* (Bloodaxe Books, 2008) won the T. S. Eliot Prize. Her third poetry collection, *Byssus*, was published by Picador in early 2014. She is currently Writer in Residence at Glasgow University and Glasgow School of Art, supported by Creative Scotland.

Canan Marasligil is a freelance writer, literary translator, editor and curator based in Amsterdam. She specialises in contemporary Turkish literature as well as in comics. She has worked with cultural organisations across wider Europe and has participated in a wide range of residencies. She is the creator of *City in Translation*, a project exploring languages and translation in urban spaces.

Malika Booker is an writer whose work is steeped in anthropological research and rooted in storytelling. Her writing spans poetry, theatre and installation. She was the inaugural Poet in Residence at the Royal Shakespeare Company and a Fellow of both Cave Canem and The Complete Works.

About the Poetry Translation Centre

Set up in 2004, the Poetry Translation Centre is the only UK organisation dedicated to translating, publishing and promoting contemporary poetry from Africa, Asia and Latin America. We introduce extraordinary poets from around the world to new audiences through books, online resources and bilingual events. We champion diversity and representation in the arts, and forge enduring relations with diaspora communities in the UK. We explore the craft of translation through our long-running programme of workshops which are open to all.

The Poetry Translation Centre is based in London and is an Arts Council National Portfolio organisation. To find out more about us, including how you can support our work, please visit: www.poetrytranslation.org.

About the World Poet Series

The *World Poet Series* offers an introduction to some of the world's most exciting contemporary poets in an elegant pocket-sized format. The books are presented as bilingual editions, with the English and original-language text displayed side by side. The translations themselves have emerged from specially commissioned collaborations between leading English-language poets and translators. Completing each book is an afterword essay by a UK-based poet, responding to the translations.